## Praise for *Going There*

The poems of Max Heinegg's *Going There* redefine what it means to arrive. When the beauty of a memory guides us toward new meaning. This is such a moving book! With brilliance and tenderness, Heinegg's poems take us, over and over, out to where "love's waiting."

**Christopher Salerno**, author of *The Man Grave*

Max Heinegg's new collection offers many one-page windows into his home, through which the single-reader can spy a man making his way through life as a father, a husband, a teacher, a hard-working man on holiday, a son who's lost his father, or found his grandfather in Rome. While women are today well-served, young men have few enough models for how to be a post-patriarchy adult male, and this poet's way of living out his years is tender, moving, and exemplary. The metrically-controlled meditations often work by an arrangement of mirrors, the older man reflecting on his boyhood, the husband seeing himself in his wife's eyes, the father seeing flashes of his own youth in his growing daughters. Throughout, there's a sense of the music of words at play, which comes easy to a poet who can still find his old groove as a rock-and-roll singer.

**Adrian Frazier**, member of the Royal Irish Academy, professor emeritus at the National University of Ireland, author of *The Adulterous Muse: Maude Gonne, Lucien Millevoye and W.B. Yeats*

# Going There

Max Heinegg

LILY POETRY REVIEW BOOKS

Copyright © 2023 by Max Heinegg
Published by Lily Poetry Review Books
223 Winter Street
Whitman, MA 02382

https://lilypoetryreview.blog/

ISBN: 978-1-957755-24-3

All rights reserved. Published in the United States by Lily Poetry Review Books.
Library of Congress Control Number: 2023938688

Cover art: John Gallaher, "Also Going," digital collage, 2023

*For my father*

## Table of Contents

### I

1. The Wizard
2. For Vera Rubin
3. Left Behind
4. Sunrise in Tulum
5. Father's Day
7. Loveliness
8. Hive
9. Across the River
10. True
11. Memory's Alchemy
12. Ava at 13
13. Raspberry
14. The Robin
15. Singing in Cursive
16. These Fall Sundays
17. The Buck
18. The Concord Trees
19. Zoo
20. Dancing in the Gardens of Stone
22. Waiting for Bono
24. Dear Thalia Z.
25. Grace
26. Fireroad
28. Fells by Morning
30. Wayfinder

II

33  Afterlife
34  Lines at Center Falls
35  Children's Hospital
36  Post Crisis, We Promise
37  Eminent Domain
38  Feeder
39  Lendings
40  Picking Crab
41  The Vulture
42  Cathedral
43  Attendance
44  Rockport Gulls
45  Bioluminescence
47  At the Baths
48  Red Peppers
49  Between the Bars
50  Snake in the Grass
51  Spiders on the Hancock
52  Robert Johnson
53  Elegy for Jim Mouradian
55  The Long Run
56  The Pallbearers
57  Elegy
58  Rejoinder

60  *Acknowledgements*

*"I see, sweet sir, / You go where you say you'll go!"*
—the Pearl Poet, *Gawain and the Green Knight,*
translated by John Gardner

# I

## The Wizard

Nothing stands in the way of your seeing
except getting there, past the monkeys
on the wing, past capitalist deceit,
past teleology. Sure, age makes you think
it's a direction worth heading,
the wind at your back because friends know
the way, or that there's music for the tin
& leonine. Your little dog too
wants the journey, but the real question
of home isn't in the clicking
or trying to forget the toes curling
under the foundation. Death is king,
but no one is wisest.
We breathe smoke & shape our reflections
in a liar's mirror. Help him find peace
with weakness & age. Let control control
nothing. Trade one world for another.

## For Vera Rubin

*Astronomer who proved the existence of dark matter*

Who looked past the luminous to find in shadow
why contrary bodies spin at the same speed
when at its locus, love agrees, the distance doesn't
train what we orbit—what we follow does.
Planets & stars, heaviness, mass beyond measure—
she saw the universe's unaccountable darkness
& named the matter: that ten to one, the stars are
*halo* on a missing angel's body.  She divined
the inside spins elliptically, the same icy pace as out,
galaxies formed & thrown into shape by the mystery,
a potter's wheel whirling for the kiln of darkness,
where men stop short of gathering in visible
circuits of space, too busy mapping the familiar
hierarchies by twilight, naming the stars after themselves.

## Left Behind

*After a photograph by Janet Milhomme*

What became of the boy that summer,
biking up the road that the town built over
is the way a child sees enormity
where there is none. Believes the road
is a way out of childhood, a place no child wants
to be seen, the public face now temperament,
the start of what they call our nature.

Forty years since I saw him ducking
through the neighbor's half-yard,
the garage window smashed by a Doc Gooden
impression, fleeing to delay judgment,
which would only be a note of apology.

In the small town where his grandparents would die
quietly, the boy stands in black & white & stares,
several feet from the curb in a Charlie Brown shirt,
at the edge of a drying wood, a half-sidewalk.
There are rarely any cars to worry him.
It's summer, & he spends evenings in
his uncle's old single bed
reading Reggie Jackson's autobiography,
wondering at the feeling of *high cotton*.

In the photograph, I read his eyes say,
*Come, let's go*, past this context like a chrysalis,
& leave the branch quiet outgrew,
the inside once a world.

## Sunrise in Tulum

Winter crests on a sliver of beach
as everything rests on rosettes
of pink moss, & the sky is Maya
blue above the mountain of sea.
Backs to the waves, teens crank
mumble-rap, the eternal insufficient.
Then they rouse for cartwheels, sparkling
for each other, as old heads turn
to their laughter, the sun now breaking
clouds that cling to the Caribbean.
At their age, I was shown the Grand Canyon
& was bored by the miraculous rust.
My father sighed, then aimed
his camera towards the rim.

## Father's Day

In the weeks after my father dies,
I see him everywhere alive.

The man that left me, mistaken
for gone-out-walking white haired men

who laze on benches, craning forward
to nose their menus, fretting orders—

who stand to read the news aghast
& lean into their arguments,

riveted to invisible worlds.
I'm assured by every echo of

that voice. I follow wherever
I can hear it, into the hearsay

of the leaves, into my limited
future, into philippics of wind,

into a too-late eulogy,
as if the half a century

I was given to learn the secrets
my father guards were insufficient

to see his failures truthfully.
Even as I dream I hold his body,

(his eyes diving out of his mind,
my arms stronger for the dread)

I know he is gone. The form no longer
an actor, or the world a stage for

an audience that does not want to be
here. I would give anything to leave.

## Loveliness

When I return, she's stitched
orchid redolent cloves into oranges,
dipped the perfumed circle in the violet
of orris root & tucked amber apples
in mountain laurel. It's Christmas
& the humble orange is now *pomander,*
more than it was by adornment,
though less than that once sought gift.

She remembers scents' protection,
burns beeswax in a service of fire,
wards illness away with air. In her absence,
I'd lock the windows & rove bottles'
squalor, flop in a hopeless apartment.
Perhaps. I buy safflower for our rice,
hibiscus to color my brews & Elixir
guitar strings. Guilty pleasures escape

judgment when no one else judges.
Friends will say we've spent too much,
but Teasdale's right: *Spend all you have*
*for loveliness & never count the cost.*
All of our debt has been delicious,
& all the magic I once doubted
of domestic alchemy says, If you can,
cast for changes, never let the lead stay.

## True

She admits to lying, all those years,
about loving my body as it fell
from level. Happier, today she sees the oak
fall in the yard & calls for a woodsman
to carve a chest to keep costume jewelry,
birthday notes from our daughters,
love's reminders I honor the family rule:
use what you have. My luck—
the old shed's flooded with all but saws,
hammers & axes—the children have our money,
& bare hands can't smooth a splintered face—
but I've got a basement, bench, & dumbbells.
Lonely to burn as all that wood, I know
enough to lift for leverage. Love's waiting.

# Hive

*That which is not good for the beehive cannot be good for the bees.*
—Marcus Aurelius, *Meditations*

We defy the rule of change
beneath the same imperious skies
Aristotle once took our queen
for a king   thinking we lifted our sons
& daughters from the same flowers.
The philosopher's dust, but the hive stows on,
as you court monoculture, we are more
& more our brothers' coroners. Absence
reminds all that must be kissed to kiss back:
almond, coriander, apricot. The wind will
remember us as pollen's porters, clever
guests who saved, sip by dram, to pour the last
in a trembling of wax. Our workers' royal
jellies stuffing every little one's room with fuel,
teeming winter's sleepy hexagons of sage,
fireweed, basswood—tastes the earth gave us
six weeks enough for wings,
bows rosined up by the sun.

## Across the River

On La Grand Roue de Montréal, I remember
20 years ago, when we first stayed in Old Port,
how the irate Quebecois bombed the Second Cup
for putting signs in English. No one would speak to us,
but we drank kir royales with Alex near McGill, ate pastrami
sandwiches at Schwartz's & enjoyed the difference
of the exchange rate. Without children, we drank wine
at Le Paris, lounged in our hotel & rented skates here.

Today, our car stops at the acme of the arc.
*Someone* didn't want to see the Aztec exhibit at the Museum
of Anthropology. *Someone else* did,
but there's no frustration now. *We* changed.
At this moment it means Stella, looking down to find
her sister & mother by the maroon of their parkas, skating
the strip of the St. Lawrence by the closed zipline
to the edge of the bridge, while the Olympic rink is
emptied for the zamboni to slowly glaze the ice.

Above Old Port together, I point to Jesus & she to City Hall,
recalling where we've eaten & where we've parked.
Perhaps because I'm quiet, she decides to start talking
about a boy, says she knows what they are like.
Your father was once a boy, *imagine the distance
he had to cross*, I tell myself. The old life like the river
of ice that seems eternal seen left to right,
though cut across, it's quick
passage, even briefer as it's told.

## Memory's Alchemy

In the 23rd hour, the cord knotted, a devil's scarf
only a scalpel could loosen. Her heartbeat
swan-dove the screen. You never saw,
as I did what the birth class taught:
say *I love you*, then   shut   the   fuck   up!
Once we signed, determined nurses spirited
you into Delivery. As I waited outside, absurd
in elastic booties, my hallway walk became
steps one takes in dreams to a field of entire light
before a sea where two drowning swimmers are
pulled, shuddering. Then surgeons turned seraphic,
& the bloodied, counted towels vanished.
The simple bed became the frame
where forty-two weeks of the leaden ended, &
our life nested in a rest of gold.

## Ava at 13

She lets her sister be served first, doesn't hover
as I take down the candles. I'll want to remember
this patience in the photograph, not you & me
worried out of the frame, probably marking
the party we put on. Tonight, before the dark
stifles any tears, I admit we have five years,
depending on interest. You talk saving for what
memories we can afford, but what did we ever want
from our parents except knowing they were
at our performances. You dread the possible
distance, promise to follow her, readying shawl
& yarn. I've got my guitar, *George & Martha*
to read them. Say the word, daughter, we'll sell
the door's gold-hinges, the garden's good dirt.

## Raspberry

This is what I left the city for—
a sight to soak in, the *ah*
in yard, a pint in a palmful,
the fruit that grows itself.

In summer, when they sit
heavy, loose to the touch,
I yield to ants that drag a crown off,
& wait until a thin pinkie can
don the knit pink hat, then focus
& get at the fractal of

drupelet a fat lip,
level an igloo's row,
sepal a present's bow,
peduncle a bristling

the tongue plays lazy
pestle to, molars for
mortar. Seeds bitter-
sweet as the month is
plucked. One, not done.

## The Robin

Brambles scraped me when I freed him
from the garland's noose of silver
tinsel wire, caught behind the beak,
an old wreath's gift the wind believed
should float toward new happiness.
He'd sought the bauble for his nest
to decorate the dog rose shade
where he had kept a thorn perch safe
enough to settle into singing.
I lifted him by his flint wings,
as ants descended his black throat.
What does the sunshine say about
fortune if the symbol of spring
is hanged in search of shimmering?

## Singing in Cursive

My daughter mocks the radio—
the lover who drags his lyric
through the notes & leaves
no space between. The growling
bleeds into a weeping she
says is *extra*, each syllable's
showboat slink toward smooth
indecipherability. She says Halsey
mostly, but boys also make it
labor to interpret what might be
sidewalk pleas because no game,
resigned dreams or drunken well-
wishing after love's eviction. Maybe
anamnesis is the way a 14-year-old
could know sans experience that
losses are meant to be sung clearly,
in words that do not cling to brittle
melody, an air you do not want to hear
yourself, beautiful only to someone else.

## These Fall Sundays

Daughters, don't write autumn,
& I won't edit this later to Bon Iver. Plaintive
is not a compliment if you've got it good.
Virtue depends on limited complaints.

The death of ego is benediction.
Lucky man to crank the Verve a bit
in the AM. Admit, I never *really* drank, but
when I did, I quit short of ruin.

Sleep on, family. Savor it. I'll resurrect
that 50s version of Dad who skips self-pity, rising
for groceries to be imagined breadwinner.
Digging my return, after dawn, the open road's

the kind of freedom a father revels in
sans guilt. The morning light glimpsed alone
is less than the light falling through evening
together, our years fair trade for aging, &

love our justified distraction. So what
I did was nothing that you wouldn't
do, that you won't love to, &
I wish you no regret in your discovery.

## The Buck

I'd heard the King of Oak Grove wanders
headstones by the tombs, but I'd never
met the monarch. Mid-run, pace

aligned to heavy metal
drums, my steps cemented
when he rose, unheralded.

Traffic genuflected, then
leaned, lurched forward. He stood
lofty, staring down his train

in the morning road, buckling
commuters. All our pleasure
to see him then remember

power, crossing the center
lane's yellow stripe in seconds,
red in his robe, oak shoulders,

bole for a midriff, white throat,
antlers bone branches. All through
with his audience, he leaped

to preserved forest
that shades nobility so well,
only the symbols stay.

## Concord Trees

In the spring calligraphy,
honeysuckle's invitation,
buckthorn's warning.

Also, a sign by the irises: Thoreau,
& longing after meaning, a bridge
well-kept, the dead beneath.

The museum is closed now, but the oak
trunk's slashed initials still assert
youth's admirable damage,
connections likely ended
here. The romance sleeps
in its scars, the dragon-paw roots
gouge the shoulders of the road,
& loom like indignant mines
you have to look out for yourself.

## Zoo

Suicidal boys try the door to the polar bear,
who twists a 20-gallon bin into a chew toy.
Seeing this, little hands slap the glass harder,
knocking on a world that would not tolerate
such puny masters. Their mothers call after
them, holding them at a visible distance,
as they discuss recipes, wondering aloud
if returning to their jobs is a good idea.
*Get the hell out of the house!* My wife says, *All
that eating & shitting & cleaning kills your mind!*

In another enclosure, a boy sits plugged in,
humming along to the bars, hardly
noticing his peers, sweet-seeming tweens
who knuckle to rouse the alpha,
a 550-pound sage, who chews on romaine
& quiet. We all wait for the potential
to become kinetic—at last, we luck
out to see him when he crosses, massive,
effortlessly acrobatic, stronger than all
of us. Penned, but not entirely.

## Dancing in the Gardens of Stone

1.

*After a film by Parviz Kimiavi*

The slender dervish lifts the rock to his lips,
sways. In the low, parched trees,
he cradles each in the phone wires he cuts
off his neighbors' lines to make strange
necklaces of the branches. His children sold
their deaf father's garden as a stage for faith,
his turning a mystic's ecstasy, lissome arms
channeling what paying pilgrims seek,
the desert invitation.

2.
In 1990, I wandered a bazaar in Albany, NY
before the Knick for the message of The Dead.
Celebrants in open air, the spinners'
Waterhouse hair, altered followers after a *miracle*
I wouldn't part with, not for blotter acid or
psalms of smoke. Outside their circles, a voyeur
of closed-eyed whirlings meant to be observed—
they taped the seance of *Drums / Space*, waiting
for Jerry's sermon to bless *the eyes of the world*.

3.
Sundays, I pass the visible church, the living
picture of our town's wanting, unsure if it is weeds
or wheat, hoping shows will grant an audience

in God's seventh day mind. I know our garden's
no place a wanderer would one day call a shrine,
the slate we stole from a retaining wall
to make a base for outdoor fires, the rest sculptures
my love haloed with a barrel's ring. Faith is a moving
silence, the open secret of our solid dust.

## Waiting for Bono

When Kevin the carpenter told Simon of Cork
he'd heard from a friend who worked security
for The Lads when they came through town
that we might see Bono at arm's length,
we were off, Simon's sedan peeling
down Playstead to Davis Square

to admire the doorway in the Burren's back-room.
It was as fair a chance as any, a night off
for the band between a stand in the Garden—
a habit of theirs to thrill lucky punters
& my wife said, *What if you don't go & they do?*
One said, *Unlikely*

they'd pass this way, a publican's ruse,
confiding that Bono, that merchant of justice,
was nursing a broken arm from a busted affair,
*Bicycle accident? Load of shite.*
So we stood for hours, gents
trading pints, the opening call of "The Miracle

of Joey Ramone" led by Kevin, who'd seen him
twenty times, from North of the neck
of Ireland to Gillette.
All night, we kept our eyes on the backstage rope,
keeping us from no one but the bouncer
who stood at attention, careful enough

to preserve the possibility of the imminent
performance, while the barmen struggled to keep up.
Though Bono was a no-show, it didn't matter,
as the speakers streamed the hits, the crowd sang
each line, from the feminist nod of *on your knees, boy*
in "Mysterious Ways," to the gutsy empathy

of "Sunday Bloody Sunday," just
the way they do on the arena floor, full-throated
strangers, shoulder to shoulder, with beers & joints,
glowing phones proof of need & presence.
We'd find him later, maybe next summer, when we heard
he might make his way back through town.

## Dear Thalia Z.

Fingers in the lint of the Internet's purse,
I find you thirty years ago, edging axes with Chris,
whisper to grit on TT's house 58,
the sound of Come as reverie. *Now we sing
so softly, deeply* into the afterglow
of youth's loadout, oil-lipped from Hi-Fi, lit
on well whiskey & the dust of the stalls, bullshitters
on Brookline St. wheeling combos & half-stacks
into the Sound Museum at 2AM, ears feeding back,
pockets lined with ones, resolved to a feathered
minor chord. Ah, for the long-swept ashes
to burn again. Your songs remind me
of nights I thrilled but readied to end,
*waiting for the pillow to cradle my head.*

# Grace

*For Jeff Buckley*

I was a busboy swapping ashtrays when I heard
a soprano in the basement of the Fez, NYC,
climbing octaves like a valkyrie. A singer
myself, I traded my shift, saying
it was for second-floor tips—
when the audience emerged from the stairwell
like they'd seen the loveliest ghost.
When he signed my Nietzsche, young
& knowing, he wrote, *May you be luckier
in love.* We lost the leaf, but we were.

# Fireroad

*for Chris Whitley*

What can we keep clear of all that catches?

I found a fireroad wide enough
for engines to reach the reservoir.

Listen to the songs of containment.
From one measure of ash, from one refrain,
a secular blessing drifts, granted.

As I leave the night fire, I trust
it won't catch on the rug's edge.
We've no wings to rise above a blaze &
no nest but this.

At Bill's Bar on Lansdowne St.,
he was skeletal in a white tank top,
his resonator a beacon,
cigarette tucked behind the guitar nut,
"Little Torch" an easy fire
*fanning out her flame to little men.*

After the show, I dared
"*Dirt Floor* is my generation's *Pink Moon*,"
rehearsed, finger on my lighter.

Absent of faith, find the burning bush
in singers, call them conduits, fan their souls,
but warmed, let them smolder,
absent air, consumed.

In the space that waits for grace notes,
the bluesman captured floating verses,
tuning to himself, sliding from the Bowery
to Belgium, from *Big Sky* to Berlin.

In his bowler hat, in mid-day Vermont foot-stomps,
his voice kept vigil;
the National steel sang a *scrapyard lullaby,*
& swept the *dirt floor,* kept it clear.

After love & the cells sicken,
the things we wanted for ourselves
sleep in fire's forgiveness,

the living trace maps in the ash.

## The Fells by Morning

I chase my neighbor, the devout
Mennonite, into the Fells
each morning for five miles, before
he bikes fifteen to work. He lets me know,
as I struggle to keep pace
up the gravel paths that reconnect
the preserved land after the road
divides, that *anyone who doesn't believe
the Bible is the revealed word
of God is in a social club.*
I admire his rigor,
but where he thinks the Word is
divinity, I think it's the world
that is revealed, the manifestation
of what I would call holy. Still,
he teaches me persistence:
the way he stands outside my door
at six sharp, rain falling
or not, dragging me under
the canopies, along the reddish,
pine-needled floor, soft underfoot,
as we follow a small rocky stream,
past a flat swamp, up Ram's Head,
and then the restricted path
we run through, the fireroad
to the reservoir, talking
Dostoyevsky, how he couldn't fathom
a mind like Raskolnikov's,
how for him, though thoughts
may lead you to trench or abyss,
it is where we choose to follow
that defies madness, defining us.
As we run, him leading, improvising
trails when I'm exhausted, tacking on

another half mile when his GPS fails,
neither of us with water, I learn
resistance. Hung-over most mornings,
I accepted his discipline as deserved
medicine. I envied his direction,
he never had to brace himself,
as with what can the faithful collide?
I followed, missing the scenery
to avoid knotted roots,
staggering after grace.

# Wayfinder

*In Reykjavik*

The mother of the goldsmith shows me the rune
beside the protective eye of awe
near the lava stone & silver necklaces
adorned by the carved teeth of whales.

She says, *Here is the wayfinder*
& puts it on so I may imagine
how it will look on you.

Along the walls, she has modeled
her son's creations. In black & white,
a grandmother, still beautiful.

I hope this is where we may follow,
the way an older culture set
the symbol to stay in one place,
offering
something of the earth
that skill has shaped, clasped
with a magnet to hold the rope, so
you will know where you are going
even when you don't.

II

## Afterlife

At the border, our presence was questioned
& deigned justified. We drove on
to find the City of Saints
through a barren hour of fields, then odd
rows of tiny Christmas trees
beside family farms' closely joined
silos in winter sun & the tragicomic
temperature. Despite, birds gathered
to share the cold or taunt the hardy
conception of ourselves, the American myth
workers endure for Heaven's reward—
the Greeks told normal souls they were
destined to become leaves, flitting
in the grey meadows of Asphodel,
unsettled by wind. Weakling shades
not dark enough to warrant Furies'
whips or any depth of Tartarus,
& not the warlike bright who died
without dying to sleep in the Elysian
Fields beneath their own constellations.
Just leaves who take the name of shades,
& worst, no memory—the streams of Lethe
steal everything. There's no keeping
the look you're giving, the one
that took my life to see.

## Lines at Center Falls

The way water abrades
    the pane of itself
to leave the ice behind

    like a snake, scraping
the rasp of a fallen branch
    to unflesh from its dead

coil. For now, the clock tower pins
    the hour on the hill above.
Time is the skin we all must slip—

    from youth, I fevered free.
Older, I would keep within
    scales that clutch the body.

## Children's Hospital
*May 2020*

The princess is bedecked in sweat,
the wires flow out of walls.
Blood flecks her gown by her left arm,
the heart monitor frogs.

Sandpaper gasps outside the door,
a gaunt boy on a gurney.
Her room's small clock, its tiny sink,
child-sized ceremonies.

Outside, the night deliberates,
reprieve is all I ask.
The morning nurse arrives to read
the verdict to us, masked.

## Post Crisis, We Promise

After the children balked, autonomous, we knew
they were making permanent memories. So,
we corked it, admitted ten years *had* got behind us.
Age had made us less courageous—all-too-busy
staving winter cave-minds with six-second hugs,
buying Darn Toughs to be warm in our Docs,
Dodging their daily radar, whipping off tablecloths
to shock ourselves with what we could pull off.
By night, though, there was nothing to regret.

Love was the remarkable escape we had made,
a tale that improved every time with the telling:
how a lamplit past was once a black ice road
we'd barreled through with no GPS because Mom
always had a map. One day, we'll go West,
our money *right*, laughing after labor's fiasco,
tilting our ladder toward torrential light,
headed into the canyons with full canteens
for Arizona to burn the sourness out of us.

# Eminent Domain

When it wants, the silent government will
seize the building—from the joists of my bones
to the bed of your breath, the electric to the outlets.

The spaces our souls once stood in to hear
the blood spark in the song will be theirs, & in that openness,
they'll redirect the crude, re-route the highway

or raze a single-family's foundation to frame a mansion,
or just sell the dirt. With nowhere to be buried, we'll
agree to be ash, & they'll take our smoke for signature.

Powerless, we'll wear pride less like a mantle than proof against
the flames & after, when shades come to show where
the phoenix teaches the only trick worth learning,

how the clothes of death are just a costume change—
will we become skeletons that won't terrify?
For now, love is this link on the great chain

hammered to be heard, & the alarm from a sleep we are
damned to forget. Forgive us this stay beneath the sky,
the years spent begging them not to take it all away.

## Feeder

Are the spirits for us
the way we are
for the birds

at the window, waiting
for their feast to be
our pleasure.

On the perch of
the seed hoard, morning
doves tolerate the cardinal,

& the junco stays one
wing away from the finch.
Or is watching the earthbound

boredom? All our territorial
pecking without flight, plumage,
like the squirrel, hanging upside-down

to crack a plastic but engineered safe?
Do the spirits see our failure so?
Can such effort be ignored?

The way his limber brilliance
curls around the stems,
failing to break in.

# Lendings

> *Off, off you lendings*
> *—Lear*

Fools as well for all this wanting
to feel the sea-wind crack
its cat o' nine tails, for daring
*let me have it* instead of waiting
out, for howling, gone with the breath
needed to companion the hours,
welcome as fire's ceremonial pace,
limbs that shouldered winters
ash in this backwards alchemy,
life's beauty is strange as silk
from which we weave but will
not keep, glad in truth
for any hand-me-down to bear
this storm or the one to follow.

## Picking Crab

Stripped of his armor, the crab's still admirable.
Micah reminds me not to pull too quickly—
the big claw's best broken slowly.
Its translucent blade of cartilage brandishes
a hollow threat, still a gesture I respect.

This largesse once joined the *bugs*
he calls *loppers*, sideways walkers
who crossed the trap's kitchen to the parlor,
baited by racks of the same silver & blue sea
herring they scour the rocky bottom for.

He's done the brunt already, boiled both cancers,
the Jonah & the Rock, removed the plate,
brushed away the *dead man's fingers*, saved me
admitting I don't want the tomalley.
I cheat further with scissors & roll a pin

over the barbed legs, thin damp
chambers, shells clinging to the flesh. Salty
nutcrackers & picks menace the broken
exoskeleton. This hour for ounces,
jaded by fragments, after the lump sum.

## The Vulture

> *But I am old and you are young*
> *And I speak a barbarous tongue.*
> *—Yeats*

I tried to warn them, but from my beak
they would receive nothing. They saw baldness,
but that was adaptation. The building seethes

in the winter, freezes in the fall.
They took our committee for a wake,
pleasant voices for gospel, but when it's drought,

the wall writes itself. From one who grieved
her mother too long, one for being gay,
one who couldn't skip Bonnaroo, one Ivy

who couldn't hack it, one naive who drove
girls home, & one unkempt who sat dutifully
but too sour with his charges, meals to pick clean.

The feathers from their affections: biographies,
anthologies, DVDs, tape rolls, ballpoints,
ancillaries, master texts I'd shadowed over.

Flesh to digest before they whet another veteran.
I let my brood claw the marrow: markers,
copy paper; teaching them remnants

of the habitat are fuel for ones who know
the season's scarcities; shred the remainder
without sentiment. This is how our desert divides

& will again in August, as clean-winged
fledglings settle in to make a home of it.
Their dreaming will be my inheritance.

## Cathedral

Florence, the blasted speakers I skimped on
        distorted & I heard *waves*
instead of *where    you cannot breathe,* the ocean
        a lover who never wanted to hear any prayer
save its own.

As I drive in, your echo but an octave lower, I'm pulled
        the way I imagine faith could be
followed, the way my love beckons
        me into water where she's assured, & I come to

believe our ashes will stay, here where she tells me
        to pour them, if I have to hold their strange exhalation,
& again, this light will come through the stained
        glass of the waves, our time together, the cathedral

written in images so the faithful could read
        when death was the secret everyone kept
telling, my finger taps the hymnal to hear
        the impossible, *never let me go.*

Attendance

All the mornings like burnt offerings,
raising smoke to entice fickle deities
but mainly wasting what a child
could not do without. All my charges
dreaded numbered days—I kept pleasant
count. Especially in the testing rooms,
tucking laptops into sleepy carts,
I saw how futility usually dressed,
how any welcome is forgiveness
in a bad room, to never sit
if you want peace. Between lessons,

we traveled on the calendar, paid airlines
twice to do so. The sands were everything
we needed them to be. Then, we charted
nothing. We attended to the speeches
of our children. Between the months,
they grew, seismic. My love & I aged
into a calm, the kind no one calls
romantic, but peace is a transcendence
that isn't told, as much as escapes
a record that tallies only absence.

## Rockport Gulls

Perhaps the slithering is not the black snake
sunning itself on the tramway track,
maybe it's the crickets, leaping unstuck
keys of a push typewriter. Our children stutter-step
over splinters on the wood ramp, catch balance
on the turntable, & eye where one lighthouse parapet
tumbled a hundred fifty feet out of the blue.

On the thin trail, briars on the margins,
sickening tent caterpillars billow, & at our feet,
air crunches from gull & fish bones beside poison ivy,
a combustion of red ants in the grass, near one splayed
in rotten humility. *Dead bird singing in the light of day...*
the science teacher's gallows humor, & her fisher-
man's comfort with death's ubiquity. Ocean swirling

around us, the rope with random buoys on it hardly
mark the cliff—one would survive the fall, but be mangled,
& the swarming gulls are a white cloud come down
on the fishing boat, so many the men in wisdom don't even
swat at them—they do not guard as much as own the gate-
way between the world we inhabit & the world as it will
be without us, if the island's indication, all stench

& hunting. The air-brushed bone my child snags as souvenir,
& in the berry-bushes, the eggs we should know to avoid.
Here, the gulls catch us. Full-throated & snarling, they block the path.
Later, loitering, we fish mackerel where the recent Great White
was tagged, & wonder at the paddle-boarder on her return,
a brazen quarter mile from the seal colony. How she trusts
indifference allows her return or doesn't know what follows.

## Bioluminescence

By night, through dark mangroves,
we match our strokes to the mild haunt
of coquis & coconuts falling, following

our kids' canoes & our old friends laughter
at the guide's mischievous invocation
of *Chupacabra!* the vampirical goat-sucker,

keeping the darkness light. We pause
in the center of Laguna Grande
& drape the tarp over our tied vessels

watch our wrists get gem-lit, protists
spinning around strangeness, bothered
into beauty by hands become iridescent gloves.

We hear they live five days, brightening
but once a day, their last hours budding.
The glint of cold light at agitation, gorgeous,

but there are ghosts in the glimmer near
the lighthouse I read of in Espada's "Alabanza,"
honoring the restaurant workers in the tower.

Both blazed, remember. Yet after
Maria killed the same number, we
slept nights away, calm in the same country.

Technology made the lighthouse of Fajardo
a legend the boatman is fine without,
but we need to know what to do with this

brief light and how to respect its source.
On the return, our children before us,
our friend Daniel marvels they were only

yesterday speechless. I can tell he's crestfallen
at the way their need for him has changed.
I scan the glitter, broken on the dark surface

& tell myself brevity is what shapes
beauty. Consoled by a childhood lyric
that somehow I glow with the astral,

but looking up, we find Orion
risen in the hierarchy of light
at a distance only a story can reach.

## At the Baths

I tug at the octopus suction cup
shower mat to lie on the white plastic
covered cast iron in my grandparents' house
in hour four of my Christmas trip, sinking
to the bottom of the Roman baths—
an empire of water from a tribute of sky,

largesse of clouds to genius aqueducts,
wastage embraced, forests felled to fire
for holidays of water, two *denarii* or this tab,
stutter steps from cumulus ceilings, sounding
hypnotic veils, rings, staining, fabled air
kissed off by mountains returning to tunnels

for shoulders dripping with the daze of water's
sudden humming, the melody of what's gathered
in it: whale, wave, wind, great schools, & poets:
Ovid, Virgil, Martial, Lucan, Horace, Juvenal
saw the stone walls beading up in the great *caldarium*
as mine fell to *tepidarium*—I rose to towel.

## Red Peppers

She taught me how to prepare them, to char
the indigestible gloss, to steam them
in their own heat until the sections split
& could be held like tongues.

Near the kitchen table, the servant's stairs
led to my old room. Grandma Ethel slept in the next.
She'd return from her nursing rounds & bask
in Willie Nelson, accompanying him on accordion.

Once I happened upon her naked; I made myself forget.
Once, she took me to *Excalibur*, & draped her cold
fingers across my eyes when Guinevere found Launcelot
armored in the woods. A grudge worth years.

She wore her hair in a bun, licked her lips before speaking,
& kept cow tongues in our fridge, a terror
I never saw opened, like her feud with my father,
but I'd hear stories, when the other was gone

& wonder at what shine had been
held over the grates. The way these ornaments
cling to their scorn under cold water, the flesh
fighting to avoid tenderness, not let go.

## Between the Bars

*For Elliott Smith*

I see the person I was before walking up the steps
of that Portland bus to the carpet factory, saving

for a red-eye back to you. This was '96, after
three months of waiting by the door

for your intermittent letters. I pinned my hopes
to his music of absence, slipped into pot-addled reveries,

following roommates to the Silver Dollar's tables,
learning to break, put English on the ball, drinking

hefeweizens. Odwalla's in the morning, Camels
& that bus, braced hard against its own breathing,

the chords linking minor to minor, the melody
of each bar door opening. I hoped to find him

in Olympia, but by then, I'd missed last call.
His double-tracked voice balanced a weakness

the evening rain recorded. It's true,
what he sang: *They want you, or they don't.*

He knew young what I learned then—
being alone is no clothing in the cold.

## Snake in the Grass

An old man points it out to us
between the rails of the hotel fence:
a three-foot whipsnake, scavenger
in the morning sun, widening jaws
to down a rotting black squirrel.
*They don't unhinge,* he says, *that's a myth,*

*they only widen.* Make the necessary
change. He stretches to engage,
*I thought snakes did their own killing.*
His wife hints it's time to check out,
so he leaves with, *In the midst of life
we are in death,* & thinking Smiths

beneath my breath, I breathe *et cetera.*
That afternoon, driving Rocky Mountain
National Park's Lava Cliffs to Iceberg Pass
where the road is built into the sky,
there are no guardrails & we are offered
an epic death on either side. I stifle the fear

everyone else stomachs & wrestle free
from the voice that slithers up from the rocks
to wring my breath. I know what not to do.
By the edge, I grip the lane barely shouldered
by the ridge. The end of grief is a turn away.
Nothing as terrifying could be easier.

## Spiders on the Hancock

Steady at their webs on the brilliant edge,
Chicago spiders range outside the windows
across the 94th floor, at every vantage
their dedicated tensile silks arrayed
upon the beams, a metal of their own.
Is this occupation accident, or do they know
leaders? One pioneer who gathered
the colony for an ingenious monopoly
on the city's flies? Or squatters
on the palace as the window washers strike,
chanting below, banded for a $5 raise?
When the workers return to their bravery,
will they say *It's you or me* to the company,
or send them flying with *Happy trails, Hans*?
Even one friendly minds the clutter
of eensy-weensies shrouded on the glass,
but the view's irresistible, so we press on Tilt,
eight bays at time facing the towering facades.
Here is the corporation, & here, individuals
dangled in the overhang, a dotted line of eyes
the horizon signs left to right, from Lake Michigan
to the pinnacles, whose height affords this
hovering interest in such daring creatures,
who dying become lawsuits, beads woven *in situ*.

## Robert Johnson

The story runs he couldn't
catch a tune with a hound's tooth,
so he took his dream of delta rain
on a train to Clarksdale
& returned weeks later with a *gift*,
but the Devil prefers to receive.
Some say he was starving, so what
was the danger in parting
with his immortal soul?
A flower is wasted on a grave.

## Elegy for Jim Mouradian

I'd thought to come & see him soon.
The cold had slipped beneath the door
to pull the strings from the fretboard.

The plan itself was pleasant, good
to see him standing, holding court
on his headset, hands in his work,
tuning guitars by harmonics.

While I waited, I'd talk to Jon
in the back, beside the Gibsons,
soldering, his dog roving
beside his vintage car. We'd chat
about our kids, making music.
I'd stood this way for twenty years,
waiting my turn to talk to Jim.

He fixed them: the cracked Epiphone
with tree glue, the Guild's custom tone,
lipstick pickups for the Special,
my mother's bridgeless classical,
I'd thought to donate, but after his
touch, Segovia would've played her.

When my turn came, though I'd been away
a year, he'd call me over by name,
thank me for being a teacher;
we'd talk students, the beers he liked,
then my daughters. Saying,
*Sons are easier.*

I'd reread the sticker on the front
of his workbench before I'd leave
the instrument in his trust:
*that man's a strand within the web.*
Change changes us.

Tonight, I'll play a twelve-bar-blues,
the first chord held, the next assumed,
the last one, where I'll risk a flourish:
he was the root I once returned to.
I'd thought to come & see him soon.

## The Long Run

Along the Mystic Lakes,
I hear the scrape of shells
against the water, sculls
pulled by younger arms.

The whitest haughty swans,
lord their beauty. Look
the mile marker above,
a beehive holding on.

My body spent the last,
a paper trail of will,
I burned before midday,
my shadow gains on me.

## The Pallbearers

When my grandfather's priest swings the thurible
over him, gravity & the pendulum
prepare us for ruin, but luck intercedes:
he neither drops the censer nor taps the casket,
but when he eats the host, it crackles.

He speaks of the everlasting—his voice shaking
the ready tree, these gathered who want comfort,
even those who doubt the psalms remember
their warmth, & crossing pews to reach strangers' hands,
a noble ceremony I have missed for twenty years,

not since graduating from the kids' table
to the dining room where sherry was kept
in crystal, & we were expected
to hold hands during grace. Sundays,
he'd take us to the center of town,

& though I was no secret atheist, I admired
how the room made itself quiet for the sermon
to be delivered, the way my grandfather's
children lifted the weight of their father over
glare ice, balancing his body & our grief.

# Elegy

*For Rebecca Dobert's father, Po*

In the manner of December
trees that know they will again
be rain's familiar, not bound by
the climbing ice. The heart knows
that it is branch as well
as flower, offering into darkness
small gift for the ceremony.
If the branch holds tightly,
it is because it knows winter
reaches for the roots, & life strains
to extend in shadow. Even fallen,
the branch remembers flower. So,
love calls for you like a father,
to be sure you are there.

## Rejoinder

When we're rewound, back to the roots,
don't let them say we made of music a private matter,
a garden for no one

to enter. An audience of flowers
is its own indeed, but the rain plays a part.
The performance of soil a stage the sun admired
with a roving eye, sometimes jealous,
judgmental. Our part? A gardener knows
when to get out of the way.

Don't let them say we added nothing,
mornings dead-heading, noons filling
small wells for hostas, climbing the yard's incline
with beer for love to drink in dirty work gloves.

Instead, say we kept the gate without hinge or lock,
say we left alone what was on its own
enough. Say, we left a reminder.

## Acknowledgements:

### I

| | |
|---|---|
| The Wizard | *Sweet Tree Review* |
| For Vera Rubin | *Indianapolis Review* |
| Left Behind | *Book of Matches* |
| Sunrise in Tulum | *Muddy River Poetry Review* |
| Father's Day | *Lily Poetry Review* |
| Loveliness | *Thimble* |
| Hive | *Sweet Tree Review* |
| Across the River | *Misfit Magazine* |
| True | *Comstock Review* |
| Memory's Alchemy | *Connecticut River Review* |
| Ava at 13 | *Sweet Tree Review* |
| Raspberry | *Thrush* |
| The Robin | *32 Poems* |
| Singing in Cursive | *Kestrel* |
| These Fall Sundays | *The Adirondack Review* |
| The Buck | *Peacock Journal* |
| The Concord Trees | *Ibbetson Street Press* |
| Zoo | *Mojave River Review* |
| Dear Thalia Z. | *Nixes Mate* |
| Dancing in the Garden of Stones | *Matter* |
| Grace | *January Review* |
| Fireroad | *All Things Chris Whitley* |
| Fells by Morning | *Tar River* |
| Wayfinder | *Live Nude Poems* |

### II

| | |
|---|---|
| Afterlife | *Pirene's Fountain* |
| Lines at Center Falls | *The Inflectionist Review* |
| Children's Hospital | *Plainsongs* |
| Post Crisis, We Promise | *River Heron Review* |
| Eminent Domain | *Kestrel* |
| Feeder | *Panoply* |
| Lendings | *West Texas Review* |

| | |
|---|---|
| Picking Crab | *Nixes Mate* |
| The Vulture | *Panoply* |
| Cathedral | *Yes, Poetry* |
| Attendance | *Plainsongs* |
| Rockport Gulls | *River Heron Review* |
| Bioluminescence | *The Banyan Review* |
| At the Baths | *A Too Powerful Word* |
| Red Peppers | *Night Heron Barks* |
| Between the Bars | *Misfit Magazine* |
| Snake in the Grass | *West Trade Review* |
| Spiders on the Hancock | *Pangyrus* |
| Robert Johnson | *Mojave River Review* |
| Elegy for Jim Mouradian | *San Pedro River Review* |
| The Long Run | *Book of Matches* |
| Elegy (for Po) | *Lily Poetry Review* |
| Rejoinder | *Crab Creek Review* |

## Thanks:

My wife, Wendy, and our two daughters, Ava and Stella. Heinegg and Pfaffenbach families. The Lily Poetry Press family, especially Eileen Cleary, Martha McCollough, Tom Daley, Paul Nemser, Rebecca Nemser. It will always be an honor to be linked to Paul Nemser.

Robert Pinsky, Maggie Smith, Phil Metres, Virginia Konchan, Sean O'Dougherty, Christopher Salerno, and Adrian Frazier for the kind words about my books. Jared Harel, Sean Singer, Ashley Mag Gabbert, Brian Tierney, Robert Carr, and Adam Tavel for reading these poems and helping me improve them. Luke Johnson, Bunkong Tuon, Terry E. Carter, Michael Marks, and Todd Hearon for being poetry pals. Phil Memmer at *Stone Canoe,* Alan Catlin at *Misfit,* Alexis Rhone Fancher at *Cultural Daily,* Rusty Barnes and Heather Sullivan at *Live Nude Poems,* Hannah Lewis and Jesse Ewing-Frable at *Sweet Tree Review,* the Yetzirah community, and Megan Merchant at *Pirene's Fountain,* for supporting my work. Last, for my two earliest poetry teachers, Jordan Smith and Kit Hathaway, gratitude for showing me the path.

## About the Author

Max Heinegg is a poet, singer-songwriter, recording artist, editor, and literary critic. His previous collection, *Good Harbor*, won the inaugural Paul Nemser Prize from Lily Poetry Press. He has been nominated for the Pushcart Prize, Best of the Net, won the Emily Stauffer Poetry Prize and the Sidney Lanier Poetry Prize, and has been a finalist for prizes from *Asheville Poetry Journal, Columbia Poetry Review, Crab Creek Review, Cultural Weekly, December Magazine,* the Nazim Hikmet Prize, *Rougarou Journal,* and *Twyckenham Notes.*

As a singer-songwriter and guitarist, his last five records can be heard on Bandcamp, ITunes, Spotify, and Youtube. His latest record, *Through Traveler,* adapted 14 poems from the public domain into songs.

He is the editor and founder of Panther Cave Press, a guest editor of *Stone Canoe,* and has published literary reviews in *Rain Taxi* and *Atticus Review.*

Born in Cooperstown, NY, he lived in Schenectady, NY before moving to Medford, MA, where he has taught English in the Medford Public Schools for 25 years and is the co-founder and brewmaster of Medford Brewing Company. He is married with two daughters.

Connect with him on the web at www.maxheinegg.com

Printed in the USA
CPSIA information can be obtained
at www.ICGtesting.com
LVHW040914011023
759816LV00013B/996